POLICING AND RACE:
The Debate Over Excessive Use of Force

Jim Gallagher

ReferencePoint
Press®

San Diego, CA

© 2021 ReferencePoint Press, Inc.
Printed in the United States

For more information, contact:
ReferencePoint Press, Inc.
PO Box 27779
San Diego, CA 92198
www.ReferencePointPress.com

LIBRARY OF CONGRESS CATALOGING-IN-PUBLICATION DATA

Names: Gallagher, Jim, 1969- author.
Title: Policing and race : the debate over excessive use of force / by Jim Gallagher.
Description: San Diego, CA : ReferencePoint Press, [2021] | Includes bibliographical references and index.
Identifiers: LCCN 2020048168 (print) | LCCN 2020048169 (ebook) | ISBN 9781678200442 (library binding) | ISBN 9781678200459 (ebook)
Subjects: LCSH: Police brutality--United States--Juvenile literature. | Discrimination in law enforcement--United States--Juvenile literature. | Discrimination in criminal justice administration--United States--Juvenile literature. | Racism--United States--Juvenile literature. | Police-community relations--United States--Juvenile literature.
Classification: LCC HV8141 .G36 2021 (print) | LCC HV8141 (ebook) | DDC 363.2/32--dc23
LC record available at https://lccn.loc.gov/2020048168
LC ebook record available at https://lccn.loc.gov/2020048169

CONTENTS

Discriminatory Policing

Around eight o'clock in the evening on May 25, 2020, four Minneapolis police officers confronted a Black man named George Floyd, who was suspected of using a counterfeit twenty-dollar bill to purchase cigarettes in a nearby grocery store.

Witnesses and video evidence indicate that Floyd was cooperative as he was being handcuffed and led to a police vehicle. However, the officers had trouble getting Floyd into the car. In frustration, Officer Derek Chauvin, a twenty-year police veteran and the highest-ranking officer at the scene, pulled Floyd out of the car. Floyd then fell facedown into the street. Chauvin pressed his knee into Floyd's neck, forcing his cheek into the asphalt. Officer Alex Kueng sat on Floyd's back, while Officer Thomas Lane held down Floyd's legs. "I can't breathe man. Please! Please let me stand,"[1] Floyd begged, according to a transcript taken from one officer's body camera video.

A small group of onlookers gathered at the scene, but were prevented from intervening by Officer Tou Thao. Some videotaped the encounter, while others encouraged the officers to let Floyd up. Floyd was no threat, they pointed out, because his hands were cuffed behind his back. Several times Lane suggested that Chauvin should ease the pressure on Floyd's neck. However, Chauvin refused to remove his knee until an ambulance arrived. By that time, Floyd was not moving and had no pulse. Efforts to revive him failed, and Floyd was pronounced dead soon after arriving at a nearby hospital.

Within hours, horrified bystanders were sharing videos on social media of the roughly nine-minute-long encounter. Millions of Americans were revolted and shocked by the scene, which sparked protests throughout the United States and reignited a national conversation about policing, race, and the use of force in modern-day America.

An Ugly History

There is a long and ugly history of violent encounters between law enforcement officers and Americans of color, particularly Black Americans. During the civil rights movement of the 1950s and 1960s, many Americans were horrified by images of police officers in southern cities using fire hoses, tear gas, and ferocious dogs to intimidate peaceful marchers. Similarly, the savage 1991 beating of Rodney King by Los Angeles police officers attracted nationwide attention, renewing concerns about police brutality and leading to public protests and riots. But police violence against Black Americans continued to occur every day, in every region of the country, often without attracting public attention.

During the mid-2010s, a series of deadly encounters raised public awareness about the use of force by police, particularly in cases involving minorities. In July 2014 an unarmed Black teenager named Michael Brown was shot twelve times by a police officer on the streets of Ferguson, Missouri. Later that summer, an unarmed Black man named Eric Garner was choked to death by New York City police who suspected he was selling cigarettes illegally. In 2015 Freddie Gray died due to injuries sustained while being driven to jail by Baltimore police. In 2016 a Black motorist named Philando Castile was shot and killed during a routine traffic stop in Minnesota while his girlfriend and her four-year-old daughter were in the vehicle.

These sorts of incidents had occurred before, but social media brought greater attention to them. A video of Castile dying in his car while his girlfriend was handcuffed was viewed by millions of Americans on Facebook. Bystanders used cell phones to record Eric Garner being choked, as well as the body of Michael Brown lying on the street for hours after he was shot. Their deaths and others sparked protestors to take to the nation's streets, shouting slogans like "Hands up, don't shoot!," "I can't breathe," and "Black lives matter."

Patterns of Abuse

High-profile deaths and protests led government leaders and public health officials to begin seeking more information about the frequency of police violence, particularly when it involved people of color. Prior to 2014 there was no national database of incidents involving the use of force by police officers. Then media outlets began collecting information on such incidents and shar-

At a December 2014 rally in Washington, DC, protesters raise their hands as they chant, "hands up; don't shoot." The words and gesture have become a symbol of outrage over police killings of unarmed Black men.

ing that data over the internet. Academic researchers conducted scientific studies to determine whether there is racial bias in policing and to identify the risk factors that contribute to deadly encounters.

About one thousand Americans are killed each year by law enforcement officers, and numerous studies suggest that race is a factor in these killings. For example, a 2019 study published in the journal *Proceedings of the National Academy of Sciences* found that Black men aged twenty to thirty-five are approximately 2.5 times more likely to be killed by police than White men are. Latinos and Native Americans are also more likely to be killed by police than White men. "For young men of color, police use of force is among the leading causes of death,"[2] the study notes.

Another study found that police in California are more likely to use force against Black people than against members of other racial groups and that Black people killed by police were twice as likely as White people killed by police to be unarmed. And in a review of more than 2 million 911 calls, researchers found that White police officers responding to calls in predominantly Black neighborhoods are five times more likely to discharge their firearms than are Black police officers responding to similar calls in the same neighborhoods.

When a fatal shooting occurs, government officials often justify police actions by arguing that the officer had to make a split-second decision to protect him- or herself and others. Still, the highly visible number of fatal encounters, particularly involving unarmed Black Americans, and the friction between communities of color and the officers sworn to protect them have brought this issue to the forefront in America, forcing the nation to address its troubled past and work toward an equitable future.

> "For young men of color, police use of force is among the leading causes of death."[2]
>
> —A 2019 study in *Proceedings of the National Academy of Sciences*

When Police Officers Use Force

On October 3, 1974, fifteen-year-old Edward Garner crouched by a chain-link fence, caught in the beam of a flashlight. Memphis, Tennessee, police officer Elton Hymon had spotted the Black teen running through the backyard of a house where a burglary had been reported. Hymon ordered the teenager, who Hymon later admitted was clearly unarmed, to stop. Garner instead turned and began to clamber over the high fence.

At the time, a Tennessee law permitted police officers to use deadly force to prevent suspected criminals from running away. Hymon drew his revolver and fired, hitting Garner in the back of the head. A search found ten dollars and a purse that Garner had taken from the house. The teen was taken to a nearby hospital and pronounced dead.

Garner's family believed that the Memphis police violated Edward's civil rights by shooting him when he was unarmed. They filed a lawsuit against the city and its police department. Initially, a judge ruled against the family, determining that the state law justified Hymon's action. However, an appeals court reversed this ruling, finding the Tennessee law unconstitutional. After a decade of legal wrangling, the US Supreme Court reviewed the case.

In *Tennessee v. Garner* (1985), the Supreme Court ruled that shooting a fleeing suspect violates the suspect's rights. The court deemed the Tennessee law unconstitutional and established an important principle: that police officers can only use deadly force when the officer "has probable cause to believe that the suspect poses a significant threat of death or serious physical injury to the officer or others."[3]

The *Garner* case marked the first time that the Supreme Court considered how and when police are permitted to use deadly force. Although subsequent cases have clarified this issue, the standard established by *Garner* has been applied to every recent case involving police brutality.

When Police Use Force

Police departments are responsible for enforcing laws, maintaining order, and keeping the public safe. When laws are violated, officers are charged with investigating criminal activity and apprehending the perpetrators. Because police work can be dangerous, law enforcement officers are authorized to carry weapons and to use force when necessary to ensure that lawbreakers do not endanger others.

Federal, state, and local governments pass statutes that regulate the use of force by officers under their jurisdiction. State and local laws must meet the standards set by *Tennessee v. Garner* as well as other Supreme Court cases that protect the rights of people who are accused of criminal activity. In the landmark case *Graham v. Connor* (1989), the Supreme Court acknowledged that "the right to make an arrest or investigatory stop necessarily carries with it the right to use some degree of physical coercion or threat."[4] But the court also ruled that police officers must use only the minimum level of force required to make an arrest or end a dangerous situation. Guided by the *Graham* decision, state and local statutes allow police officers to take an escalating series of actions, as the situation warrants, to maintain order. Collectively, this series of actions has become known as the use of force continuum.

Often, the presence of a law enforcement officer may be enough to deter criminal activity. For example, a police vehicle parked by the side of the road may compel drivers to follow traffic laws. An officer on patrol in a shopping district may make people think twice about shoplifting or causing trouble. Thus, an officer's physical presence represents the lowest level on the use of force continuum.

The next step on this scale involves the officer using non-physical force, such as verbal commands, to compel a person's behavior. There are a range of approaches the officer can take. An encounter could begin with the officer asking, in a calm and nonthreatening way, to see a person's identification. If a situation becomes more serious, the officer might issue commands in a firm voice, demanding that a suspect end a particular behavior ("Stop!") or do something that the officer wants ("Put your hands on your head" or "Get down onto the ground on your stomach").

If a person does not comply with these verbal commands, the next step on the continuum allows the officer to use physical force to gain control. This level begins with empty hand control, meaning the police officer uses bare hands, but no weapons, to subdue the subject. There are two levels to empty hand control. Soft techniques include wrist holds and armlocks, as well as strikes to specific joints or nerve areas, which enable the officer to hold or restrain the person. The use of handcuffs is also considered a soft empty hand technique.

If soft techniques do not work—or if the officer believes, in the heat of the moment, that they will not work—a more physical and aggressive hard empty hand technique (punches or kicks) is permitted to subdue the person. At this level, some municipalities allow police to use special holds called neck restraints, which can render a person unconscious by compressing the carotid artery, cutting off blood flow to the brain. However, use of neck restraints is controversial because of the risk that, if performed improperly, death can result.

The presence of a police officer or police vehicle represents the lowest level on the use of force continuum. That presence is often enough to deter criminal activity.

When empty hand techniques are not enough to bring a situation under control, the next stage on the use of force continuum allows police officers to use their weapons. *Graham v. Connor* specifies that police must only use force in proportion to the threat that is presented, so there are stages of escalating force. The first stage usually involves the use of intermediate weapons, which are less lethal than firearms. The police officer may use a baton or projectile, a chemical device such as pepper spray, or a conducted energy device (often called a Taser, after a popular brand) to immobilize a resisting person. In some police departments, officers are required to warn the person before using an intermediate weapon.

If a situation reaches the point at which an officer believes the person threatens the lives of others, including the officer, the officer is permitted to use his or her firearm. Police can also shoot

The Origin of Police Forces

The modern police force evolved gradually in the United States. In colonial America, cities and towns employed volunteers as night watchers, and they paid constables or sheriffs to collect taxes and arrest debtors, thieves, and other criminals. Merchants often hired guards to protect their ships and warehouses. In the South so-called slave patrols were an early form of police force, created to control the movement and activities of enslaved people of African descent.

White plantation owners wanted to make sure that their slaves could not escape. They also feared slave rebellions, so all southern colonies had laws prohibiting slaves from leaving their plantations at night or congregating with other slaves. "The history of police work in the South grows out of this early fascination, by white patrollers, with what African American slaves were doing," writes historian Sally E. Hadden in the book *Slave Patrols: Law and Violence in Virginia and the Carolinas*. "Most law enforcement was, by definition, white patrolmen watching, catching, or beating black slaves."

The earliest precursors to the modern police force were established in large cities like Boston, New York, Philadelphia, and Chicago during the nineteenth century. By the 1880s all major American cities had municipal police forces in place. Their primary job was to keep the lower classes of American society—poor immigrants and Black Americans—in line, preventing labor strikes, property damage, and other disruptions to the economic activities of the wealthy classes.

Sally E. Hadden, *Slave Patrols: Law and Violence in Virginia and the Carolinas.* Cambridge, MA: Harvard University Press, 2001, p. 4.

a person who has already committed a violent crime and is trying to escape, under the reasoning that such a criminal has already shown disregard for human life and is a threat to others.

Constant Evaluation

When police officers respond to a dangerous situation, they must quickly determine the level of force needed to gain control and maintain public safety. Their evaluation must account for the size or strength of any suspects, the amount of resistance exhibited by those individuals, and other factors such as whether anyone has weapons or the number of bystanders at the scene.

"You're constantly processing 'how good is this going? Is this not going so well? Am I not able to control the subject? This isn't working, what am I going to do next?" explains Travis Tennill, who trains Kentucky police officers in use-of-force tactics. "In a dynamic situation when someone is actively, aggressively trying to hurt you or kill you, it's a very difficult situation to be in."[5]

Police officers are trained to classify the actions of a subject into one of four categories in order to quickly determine what level of force is appropriate or necessary. The easiest subjects for police to handle are deemed passive compliant. These subjects recognize the police officer's authority and obey verbal commands. A passive resistor refuses to follow verbal commands but does not fight back when an officer attempts to take control with soft empty hand techniques. In both cases, the officer can gain control of the situation by staying at the lower levels of the use of force continuum.

An active resistor is a subject who does not obey the officer's commands and resists when the officer tries to take physical control. However, the active resistor fights back in a defensive way; this is a person trying to break away from officers or otherwise elude capture. Hard empty hand techniques and intermediate weapons are often necessary to subdue an active resistor. Active aggressors are not just trying to get away, they are trying to hurt or kill the police officer or other civilians. If intermediate weapons are not effective, deadly force may be required to protect the officer and the public from an active aggressor.

Thankfully, officers do not regularly need to resort to deadly force. Studies show that more than 90 percent of police officers go through their entire careers without discharging their weapons. Joseph Loughlin and Kate Flora, authors of *Shots Fired: The*

Misunderstandings, Misconceptions, and Myths About Police Shootings, write:

> Contrary to public image, officers do not wish to be in a deadly force incident and do everything in their power to avoid it at all costs, often times to their own peril. There are about 34,000 arrests each day in this country and well over 10 million a year, and in many of those arrests suspects are taken into custody safely even when many are extremely violent. Only a very small number result in shots fired.[6]

Pepper spray, Tasers, and batons (pictured) are used by police to immobilize people who pose a certain level of threat. These devices do not have the lethal force of firearms.

Defining Excessive Force

In dangerous situations, police officers often must make split-second decisions about threats and the level of force needed to maintain public safety. Sometimes, an officer miscalculates and uses an inappropriate amount of force to resolve the situation. In such a case the officer is said to have used excessive force. This is a violation of a victim's civil rights.

The frequency of excessive force incidents is difficult to estimate. According to a report published in the *Harvard Law Review*, complaints about excessive force make up about 25 percent of the approximately five thousand misconduct reports filed against American police departments each year. About 10 percent of these excessive force cases result in a civilian's death. In 2019 the Federal Bureau of Investigation (FBI) announced plans to collect data nationally on the use of force by law enforcement officers, but that database is not yet publicly available.

"Contrary to public image, officers do not wish to be in a deadly force incident and do everything in their power to avoid it at all costs, often times to their own peril."[6]

—Joseph Loughlin and Kate Flora, authors of *Shots Fired: The Misunderstandings, Misconceptions, and Myths About Police Shootings*

There is not a specific legal definition of excessive force. In *Graham v. Connor*, the Supreme Court instructed courts to consider whether a police officer's actions are "objectively reasonable" based on what the officer knew in that moment. "The 'reasonableness' of a particular use of force must be judged from the perspective of a reasonable officer on the scene, and its calculus must embody an allowance for the fact that police officers are often forced to make split-second decisions about the amount of force necessary in a particular situation,"[7] notes the court's decision.

Former Glenville, New York, police chief Mike Ranalli explains that the *Graham* decision acknowledges the danger and uncer-

tainty that police officers face in confrontational situations. "The objective reasonableness standard accepts the reality that
officers must make the best call they can
with whatever information is available to
them," said Ranalli, "and sometimes that
call will turn out to be wrong.[8]

The challenge that police officers face
is that every situation is different, and the
standard for what a reasonable officer
would do can change as soon as the circumstances change. "The moment that
you no longer present a threat, I need to
stop shooting,"[9] explains David Klinger,
a professor of criminology and criminal justice at the University
of Missouri. Civil rights attorney Walter Katz agrees. "One can't
just say, 'Because I could use deadly force 10 seconds ago, that
means I can use deadly force again now,'"[10] Katz says.

The Need for Accountability

A police officer's actions could be legal under *Graham* yet be
considered excessive or inappropriate by many people. In November 2014, for example, Cleveland
police officers Timothy Loehmann and
Frank Garmback responded to a 911 call
about a young Black man in a city park
who was pointing a pistol at passing cars.
When the officers arrived, they ordered the
man to raise his hands. Instead, the man
reached for his waistband and appeared
to be drawing a weapon. Loehmann fired
twice, and the man dropped to the ground,
fatally wounded. The "man" turned out to
be a twelve-year-old boy, Tamir Rice, with

Protesters rally in New York City on the anniversary of Tamir Rice's death. Based on legal precedent, actions by police might be viewed by the public as excessive or inappropriate while still being legal.

a toy gun. Surveillance video from a nearby building showed that Rice was shot just seconds after the police vehicle arrived.

After a lengthy investigation, an Ohio grand jury declined to indict the two officers for wrongdoing. "The evidence did not indicate criminal conduct by police," explained Cuyahoga County prosecutor Tim McGinty. "It is likely that Tamir, whose size made him look much older . . . either intended to hand it over to the

Banning Chokeholds

For many years police officers have used hand-fighting techniques known as chokeholds or neck restraints to subdue criminals or suspects who do not comply with their orders. Although these terms are often used interchangeably in the media, they refer to two distinct techniques. Chokeholds place pressure on the front of a person's neck, restricting the flow of air to the lungs. Neck restraints, or strangleholds, apply pressure to the sides of the neck, which cuts off blood flowing through the carotid artery to the brain. With either tactic, if the pressure is maintained, the subject will eventually lose consciousness. When this happens, there is a heightened risk that serious injury or even death could result.

Even before the highly publicized deaths of Eric Garner in 2014 and George Floyd in 2020, police departments in many cities were moving away from neck restraints. Los Angeles, New York, Chicago, Philadelphia, Houston and other major cities all have long-standing policies prohibiting chokeholds unless an officer's life is in danger. But experts point out that such policies have been ineffective so far. "If we look at the ban in New York City, it's kind of like a rule in an employee handbook: 'Don't use a chokehold,'" says Paul Butler, a former federal prosecutor who is the author of the book *Chokehold: Policing Black Men*. "We shouldn't expect those kinds of light bans to work."

Quoted in Monika Evstatieva and Tim Mak, "How Decades of Bans on Police Chokeholds Have Fallen Short," *Morning Edition*, National Public Radio, June 16, 2020. www.npr.org.

officers or show them it wasn't a real gun. But there was no way for the officers to know that, because they saw the events rapidly unfolding in front of them from a very different perspective."[11]

Obviously, the Rice family disagreed with this assessment. The family released a statement that said:

My family and I are in pain and devastated by the non-indictment of officers Timothy Loehmann and Frank Garmback for the murder of our beloved Tamir. After this investigation—which took over a year to unfold—and Prosecutor McGinty's mishandling of this case, we no longer trust the local criminal-justice system, which we view as corrupt. . . . In our view, this process demonstrates that race is still an extremely troubling and serious problem in our country and the criminal-justice system.[12]

The disconnect between the ways that police are legally permitted to use force and public perception of such violent encounters creates mistrust between minority communities and the police who are supposed to serve and protect them. This in turn makes the job of police officers more difficult and dangerous, since people who fear police are less willing to cooperate with them or to report crimes.

CHAPTER 2

The Militarization of Police

Shortly after midnight on March 13, 2020, Breonna Taylor and her boyfriend, Kenneth Walker, were watching a movie when they heard a noise at her apartment door in Louisville, Kentucky. Walker, who is licensed to carry a firearm, took his handgun and went to investigate. He called out, asking who was at the door, but heard no answer. Suddenly, a man wearing a black bulletproof vest burst into the apartment. Walker fired a warning shot at the unidentified intruder, hitting him in the leg. The wounded man and two others immediately fired back, spraying more than thirty bullets into the apartment. Panicked, Walker called 911 and told the dispatcher that armed men had broken into his apartment.

When the firing stopped, Walker learned that the intruders were not burglars, as he believed, but members of the Louisville Metro Police Department's Criminal Interdiction Division (CID), a paramilitary unit that investigates "violent street gangs, armed career criminals [and] criminal enterprises involving gang members,"[13] according to its website. The CID was investigating two drug dealers who were operating out of another home several miles away from Taylor's apartment. The police had been granted a warrant to search Taylor's home because she had previously dated one of the suspected drug dealers. The "no-knock warrant" allowed officers to enter the apartment without warning.

The Louisville police did not find drugs when they searched the apartment. Instead, they found Taylor, a twenty-six-year-old Black woman who worked in the emergency room of a local hospital, dying in a hallway. She had been hit by eight police bullets.

The death of Breonna Taylor, as well as hundreds of other deaths that occur during police raids each year, have raised concern about the "militarization" of local and state police forces. Over the past five decades, civilian police departments have increasingly adopted tactics, equipment, and attitudes originally developed for battlefield combat. Data indicates this new approach to fighting crime—in particular, offenses related to drug smuggling and distribution—predominantly targets Black, Hispanic, or Native Americans. The residents of these communities see the effects of militarized policing every day, while more affluent White communities may only notice it in news reports in which police departments respond to protests in armored vehicles while wearing riot gear.

Paramilitary Police

As law enforcement agencies began intercepting smugglers and arresting drug users and dealers, concerns about well-armed drug gangs led police departments to upgrade their own arsenals. Police departments in major cities used federal funding to equip and train elite special weapons and tactics (SWAT) teams. The federal government also allowed police departments to purchase surplus military weapons (including semiautomatic rifles, grenade launchers, and bayonets), armored vehicles, computers, and other equipment from the US Department of Defense for a nominal cost. Since the late 1990s, more than $7 billion worth of military weapons and equipment have been turned over to police departments across the country.

Well-armed SWAT teams were initially intended to respond to domestic terrorism, hostage situations, bank robberies, or active shooter incidents. Both police and community leaders agree that these units are highly effective at handling such events. But because such incidents are relatively rare, many police chiefs have assigned paramilitary units to other tasks, in order to justify the high cost of their training and equipment. Today paramilitary units are often deployed to raid the homes and businesses of suspected drug dealers. Local governments and state or federal courts facilitated this change in their use, upholding the legality of no-knock warrants for drug raids that permit police officers to enter homes without previously warning those inside.

According to recent estimates, fifty thousand to eighty thousand paramilitary-style police raids are conducted each year. Unfortunately, these types of raids have made it more likely that an encounter will escalate to violence or end with a fatal shooting. Drug raids involving heavily armed police officers, like the one conducted on Breonna Taylor's apartment,

A sheriff's department SWAT team takes part in a drill. SWAT teams were originally intended for use in situations involving domestic terrorists, hostages, and active shooters.

introduce violence and danger into non-emergency situations that might be handled with minimal confrontation. Indeed, police knew that the suspected drug dealer was not at Taylor's apartment at the time of their raid; he was already in police custody. "American policing today has become increasingly aggressive and, at times, even predatory," writes Jonathan Blanks, a scholar at the Foundation for Research in Equal Opportunity. "Police are incentivized to initiate unnecessary contact with pedestrians and motorists, and they do so most often against ethnic and racial minorities. Such over-policing engenders resentment among minority communities and jeopardizes public safety."[14]

The Impact on Minority Communities

As Blanks points out, the effects of militarized policing are disproportionately seen in low-income, urban communities where large numbers of Blacks or Hispanics live. This effect can be seen in the wide racial disparity in arrests and incarceration rates between Blacks and Whites. Decades of data shows that Blacks are five times more likely to be imprisoned for violating drug laws or for low-level drug dealing than Whites are, even though the rate of drug use is similar among young people of both racial groups. This is due in part to the heavy focus on policing minority communities—more arrests mean more convictions on drug charges. But it is also the result of laws that require mandatory minimum sentences for nonviolent drug offenses or that assign different penalties for possessing certain kinds of drugs. "Thousands of black men have disappeared into prisons and jails, locked away for drug crimes that are largely ignored when committed by whites,"[15] writes civil rights attorney Michelle Alexander.

Black Americans make up about 13 percent of the US population today yet account for 34 percent of the total prison

Police Work Is Inherently Dangerous

Being a law enforcement officer can be stressful and dangerous. According to data collected by the FBI, in 2019 there were nearly 60,000 assaults against police officers, with over 18,000 of those resulting in injuries. That year, 135 law enforcement officers were killed in the line of duty. Over the period from 2009 to 2019, a total of 1,627 officers were killed while on duty.

"On the whole it's much more dangerous to be a police officer than not to be a police officer," writes journalist Justin Fox. "The Bureau of Labor Statistics' occupational fatality statistics back this up: police and sheriff's patrol officers suffered 13.7 job-related fatalities per 100,000 full-time equivalent workers in 2018, compared with 3.5 for the U.S. workforce as a whole and 0.7 for those of us in professional and related occupations."

However, the number of police officers killed annually while on the job has been falling since the mid-1970s, according to a 2019 study published in the *Journal of Criminology and Public Policy*. The study's authors attributed the decline in fatalities to increased use of body armor, as well as improvements in trauma care. Enhanced training, better supervision, and new technologies were also credited for contributing to the reduced fatality rate.

Justin Fox, "How Dangerous Is Police Work?," Bloomberg Opinion, June 23, 2020. www.bloomberg.com.

population. Some try to justify this disparity by arguing that the high percentage of Black Americans living in high-crime areas means there will be more Black criminals. However, research has consistently shown that criminal activity is more closely linked to poverty than to race. In the United States low socio-economic status is the leading predictor that a person will be involved in a violent crime. The federal Bureau of Justice Statistics reports that Americans whose family incomes are below the federal poverty level, regardless of their race, are about twice as likely to commit a violent crime as higher-income Americans are. Most of the people who live below the poverty line are Black Americans, but social scientists and civil rights advocates attribute this to decades of systemic racial discrimination in housing, education, and the criminal justice system. The tactics police use, they contend, fuel the high levels of violence already prevalent in poor communities.

Little Impact on Crime

A growing body of recent research has confirmed that militarized police tactics are often both ineffective and counterproductive. Jonathan Mummolo, a political science professor at Princeton University, was able to review five years of data from Maryland, one of the few states that requires careful record keeping of SWAT activity. Mummolo found that Maryland SWAT teams were far more likely to be deployed in predominantly Black communities than in White neighborhoods. He also found that SWAT teams were used in nonemergency situations nearly 92 percent of the time. Less than 5 percent of SWAT activities involved the sort of incidents these teams were originally created to handle.

In a separate study of four years of national data, Mummolo found no evidence that the use of SWAT teams either reduced crime or increased officer safety. The data indicated that when SWAT teams were deployed, there was no statistically significant reduction in the rate of violent crime, officer fatalities, or assaults on police officers compared to less confrontational approaches. In fact, the largest effect that Mummolo did find was a strong correlation between militarized policing and community distrust of police. In several carefully designed studies, Mummolo found that when news reports publish photos of police in military gear, residents of Black and Hispanic communities are less likely to support increased police patrols in their neighborhoods. Mummolo concluded:

> The routine use of militarized police tactics by local agencies threatens to increase the historic tensions between marginalized groups and the state with no detectable pub-

25

lic safety benefit. While SWAT teams arguably remain a necessary tool for violent emergency situations, restricting their use to those rare events may improve perceptions of police with little or no safety loss.[16]

Riot Response Makes Things Worse

The negative perception of contemporary policing is reflected in opinion polls taken from 2014 to 2020 by the Pew Research Center, which have consistently found a wide disparity in views of police by Blacks and Whites. In a June 2020 poll, Pew found that 84 percent of Whites expressed at least a fair amount of confidence in police officers to act in the best interests of the public. Just 56 percent of Blacks viewed police as fair. Another poll, by the Cato Institute, found that most Black Americans believe police are too quick to use lethal force (73 percent) or that police tactics are generally too harsh (56 percent), compared to Whites (35 percent and 26 percent, respectively).

> "The routine use of militarized police tactics by local agencies threatens to increase the historic tensions between marginalized groups and the state with no detectable public safety benefit."[16]
>
> —Jonathan Mummolo, professor of politics and public affairs

The police response to the wave of Black Lives Matter protests that swept across the country during the summer and fall of 2020 may change the attitudes of White Americans, who are less likely to experience militarized policing in their own communities. Many Americans reported being shocked by viral videos or mainstream media images showing lines of heavily armed officers in riot gear knocking down demonstrators, hitting them with batons, or using tear gas to disperse large crowds.

Organizations like Amnesty International and Human Rights Watch recorded hundreds of cases in which police officers used excessive force against protestors. In New York City an officer

A Minneapolis police officer disperses protesters with pepper spray. Experts say the use of pepper spray, tear gas, and batons to break up peaceful protests can lead to riots.

pulled down the face mask of a Black demonstrator who was standing with his hands up, then blasted him in his face with pepper spray. In Indianapolis two officers shot a Black woman in the face with nonlethal projectiles and beat her with batons. Amnesty International's Ernest Coverson comments:

> The unnecessary and sometimes excessive use of force by police against protesters exhibits the very systemic racism and impunity they had taken to the streets to protest. The research shows that people who were simply exercising their human right to peacefully protest were met with such violence that they lost eyesight, survived brutal beatings, and suffered seizures and severe wounds.[17]

Most experts—including many police officers—agree that when police use force to move or disperse an unarmed crowd, a peaceful protest can quickly turn into an unruly riot. "If police

The Warrior Mentality

One aspect of police militarization is not as easily observed as armored vehicles or riot gear. Over the past five decades, police officers have often been trained to approach challenges in the same ways that soldiers do. These "warrior cops" may believe they are the only thing standing between society and chaos. This can make them view neighborhoods and streets as battlegrounds and see the people that they are sworn to protect and serve as a dangerous, threatening enemy.

Former police officer Randy Shrewsberry, now executive director of the Institute for Criminal Justice Training Reform, says:

> We are training police officers to believe that danger lurks at every corner and there's a high probability of being killed in everything you do. If we train them like soldiers, dress them like soldiers, treat them like soldiers, we can't be surprised if they act like soldiers. We give them "combat training," but where is the combat in the U.S.? There isn't any, but what we've done is set them up to view every situation as a combat situation with an enemy.

In recent years, some police academies have moved away from military-style training. Instead, they spend more time training officers in techniques that can be used to de-escalate conflicts. The goal of such programs is to train police officers to be guardians who serve and protect their communities, rather than warriors.

Quoted in Beau Yarbrough, "Are California Police Officers Trained Enough and in the Right Things?," *San Jose (CA) Mercury News*, August 9, 2020. www.mercurynews.com.

show up at a demonstration in full riot gear right away, you are projecting conflict and escalation,"[18] explains former Chicago police deputy chief Kevin Ryan.

Additionally, when riot police with armored vehicles respond to a peaceful and legal public demonstration, it sends a callous signal about that community's place in American society. Activists noted that in May 2020, Michigan State Police did not feel the need to wear any special gear while allowing White militias to demonstrate on the steps of the state capitol building against COVID-19 quarantine requirements. Officers stood calmly at attention even while the demonstrators, many of whom were armed with AR-15 rifles or handguns, yelled in their faces. Meanwhile, protesters of all races marching against police use of force against Black Americans are often met with force. "When our frustrations are met with tear gas, you're pretty much telling us it's a sin to be upset,"[19] says Aubrey "Japharii" Jones, president of a Black Lives Matter chapter in Virginia.

Ending Militarization of Police

There is no easy solution to the problem of police militarization. SWAT units are not going to disappear, since they represent the safest and most effective police response to certain highly dangerous situations, such as terrorists or active shooters. One idea endorsed by many reformers is to require departments to deploy their paramilitary units only in such situations. This would reduce the number of annual SWAT deployments from over fifty thousand to roughly four thousand per year, meaning many fewer opportunities for violent encounters.

Cutting off the supply of military weaponry and equipment represents another possible approach to the problem. During his presidential campaign, Joe Biden promised to implement tighter restrictions on federal programs that transfer military

Joe Biden (pictured at a presidential campaign event in January 2020) promised to tighten restrictions on federal programs that transfer military gear to local police departments.

gear to local police departments. Similar restrictions had been imposed by the Barack Obama administration after 2014, but they were lifted once President Donald Trump came into office in 2017.

Experts say these efforts may help, although the key to a long-term solution is improving trust between police and the communities they serve. Many believe this will require a complete overhaul of the system to require greater accountability for officers who use excessive force, as well as transparency to ensure that officers who are dismissed from their jobs for brutality cannot find another job in police work. To accomplish this, reformers believe that state governments and the US Department of Justice must implement robust programs that oversee the operations of local police and aggressively investigate and prosecute those who use excessive force. Alex S. Vitale, author of *The End of Policing*, writes:

> [The] near total lack of accountability for botched raids, excessive use of force and the dehumanization of suspects must be corrected. . . . While individual officers and police executives may be motivated by the best of intentions, as long as they continue to be the primary tool for managing social discord, poverty and even crime, we will see a continuation of the over-policing of communities of color.[20]

Retired police major Neill Franklin, the executive director of the Law Enforcement Action Partnership, agrees. "Reform is not the answer, we've been trying it for decades, and as you can see, we're just not getting anywhere," he says. "We need a new paradigm of policing in the United States. It needs to be completely dismantled and reconstructed, not changing a policy here or there."[21]

CHAPTER 3

Filming the Police

In August 2020 police officers in Kenosha, Wisconsin, responded to a 911 call in a residential neighborhood. When police arrived, twenty-nine-year-old Jacob Blake was trying to break up a fight between two women. Blake's sons, ages three, five, and eight, were sitting in his SUV, which was parked on the street.

No one is certain exactly what happened next. One witness, Raysean White, said that he walked away for a moment, and when he returned Blake was scuffling with police officers. "One of them had him in a headlock and was punching him in his ribs, the other had him in a headlock on the other side of him and was pulling his arm," White told CNN. "After they punched him in his rib, the female officer tased him and Jacob kind of leaned on the car and they proceeded to wrestle him toward the back of the car."[22] At that point, White began recording the event with his cell phone camera.

Both White's video and a second video taken by another neighbor show Blake pulling away from the officers and stumbling around the front of his SUV, trying to get to the driver's side door. Two officers are following him, guns drawn. As Blake opens his vehicle door and leans in, Kenosha police officer Rusten Sheskey grabs Blake by the shirt and fires his gun seven times into Blake's back.

Witness to Police Brutality

Despite being hit by multiple bullets, Blake survived the shooting, though doctors believed he would need numerous surgeries and would likely be paralyzed for life. As Blake lay recovering in a hospital bed, investigators with the Wisconsin Department of Justice reported that a knife had been found on the floor of his vehicle. The implication was that Blake might have been trying to reach the weapon, which would justify Sheskey's use of his firearm. However, Blake's attorney claimed that there was no knife and said that Blake was merely trying to get to his children. Raysean White and other witnesses agreed that Blake was not armed, and their videos do not show Blake brandishing a weapon or threatening the officers. Writes *Washington Post* columnist Eugene Robinson:

> The video doesn't show all of what happened before Blake headed for the car, and it's shot from a distance. But what it reveals is enough. Without this cellphone clip, I'm guessing the police report would have spoken of "noncompliance" and "resisting arrest" and some sort of "threatening move"—and that, without evidence to the contrary, Blake might have been filed away as just another Black man who got what he undoubtedly deserved.[23]

Like many other cases in which Black Americans were hurt or killed at the hands of police, the shooting of Blake sparked protests in the Black community and calls for greater police accountability. However, as Robinson notes in his column, Blake's encounter might not have drawn national media attention if it had not been recorded by civilian witnesses. Without a visual record, complaints of police brutality by Blacks and Hispanics are often dismissed or downplayed by disbelieving Whites, who typically have not had the same experiences with the intrusive, paramilitary policing methods that communities of color experience on a daily basis. But today the increased availability of video camera technology, particularly on portable devices like cellular phones, coupled with the rise of social media platforms like Facebook and Twitter, has produced a powerful tool that Black Americans hope will help hold police officers accountable.

The Right to Film

Widespread ownership of cell phones has contributed to a sharp increase in the number of videos of police encounters that are published online. In 2011 the Pew Research Center found that 35 percent of American adults owned a smartphone capable of taking photos or videos. Today that figure has risen to over 81 percent. Theoretically, this means that for every encounter involving police, there are numerous potential witnesses who can document the moment using their phone cameras. Around the country, organizations like Copwatch, Stop the Killing, and WITNESS have been formed to teach civilians how to record violent encounters in ways that are safe, ethical, and effective.

Cell phone videos and social media have become powerful tools for ensuring police accountability. This technology can help support complaints of police brutality or misconduct.

Safety is important because at times police have reacted strongly to being recorded. This was especially true during the early years of cell phone cameras, when officers would sometimes order bystanders to stop recording or to surrender their phones or cameras. More recently, most police departments have educated officers that giving such an order is illegal. Federal courts have consistently upheld the right of Americans to record police

Caught on Video: The Rodney King Beating

An infamous case of police brutality occurred in March 1991 after Black motorist Rodney King led Los Angeles Police Department (LAPD) officers on a high-speed car chase. When King finally stopped and exited his vehicle, LAPD officers shocked him with a conducted energy device then began beating him with their batons and kicking him. More than a dozen officers were involved in this attack before King was handcuffed, arrested, and taken for medical attention.

The beating and arrest might have passed unnoticed if not for George Holliday, a plumbing salesman who lived in a nearby apartment. When he noticed the commotion, Holliday grabbed his small Sony camcorder and began recording. Afterward, he informed the LAPD that he had a video of the incident, but the police were not interested in viewing it. A few days later, he gave the video to local television station KTLA, which aired it on the news. The footage was quickly picked up by national news networks, raising outrage and awareness across the country. Political analyst Julian Zelizer notes:

> Before the Rodney King video, Americans had seen images of police attacking African-Americans, but those images had primarily been from grassroots civil rights protests such as Birmingham in 1963 and Selma in 1965, or in the pictures and footage from urban riots. Rarely had they seen such graphic evidence of what many in the black community described as the routine violence at the hands of police.

Julian Zelizer, "Did the Rodney King Video Change Anything?," CNN, July 19, 2017. www.cnn.com.

officers and other government officials when they are performing their duties in public places. "The act of making an audio or audiovisual recording is necessarily included within the First Amendment guarantee of speech and press rights," commented the US Court of Appeals for the Seventh Circuit opinion in the 2012 case *ACLU v. Alvarez*. "Restricting the use of [a recording] device suppresses speech just as effectively as restricting the dissemination of the resulting recording."[24]

Although police cannot legally tell a person to stop recording, a civilian who is filming cannot interfere with an officer who is doing his or her job. This means that in certain circumstances, officers have the authority to order witnesses to move away from a crime scene. Unfortunately, some officers still use this authority to try to stop people from recording events or as an excuse to seize cameras or cell phones from witnesses.

> "Filming or witnessing can escalate a situation, and sometimes bystanders become the target of police violence. . . . No footage is ever worth your safety."[25]
>
> —Palika Makam, a coordinator with WITNESS

In some cases, camera users have been arrested for loitering, disturbing the peace, disorderly conduct, or resisting arrest when they persisted in recording video of an encounter after being instructed to stop. Although such an order might be illegal, in the heat of the moment, civilians—particularly minorities—who do not comply with police orders risk being injured themselves if officers forcibly take them into custody. Therefore, experts stress that those who film police encounters must remain respectful and calm. If they follow lawful orders, they can continue to record.

"Filming or witnessing can escalate a situation, and sometimes bystanders become the target of police violence," says Palika Makam, a coordinator with WITNESS. "The risk to your safety can depend on your identity—your background, race, gender, ethnicity, and so on—so it's important to think about whether or not you feel comfortable filming before you press record. . . . No footage is ever worth your safety."[25]

The risk does not end when the camera is turned off. People whose identities are publicly associated with recording an incident could find themselves harassed by angry neighbors or online trolls. In some cases, police themselves find subtle ways to retaliate against those who record fellow officers. Ramsey Orta, who filmed his friend Eric Garner being choked to death by police in New York City in 2014, later claimed that he and his family were tormented by local police after the video went viral. Orta was eventually arrested on drug charges; unlike Daniel Pantaleo, the officer who killed Garner, Orta spent four years in prison. Experts suggest that those who film police encounters should shield their identity, if possible, before posting a video to social media. "We've seen it can be helpful to first share your footage with a journalist or advocacy organization so that they can share the footage publicly instead,"[26] suggests Makam.

When Police Film Themselves

Video plays an important role in revealing police misconduct, but civilians cannot be relied on to film every violent encounter between police and people of color. This has led to a push for greater use of body-worn cameras by police departments. Body-worn

Body cams (such as this Axon camera worn by a Seattle police detective) are increasingly being used to provide a digital video and audio record of encounters between police and members of the public.

cameras, or body cams, are small devices that can be clipped onto a police officer's uniform and used to record digital video and audio of encounters with the public. The video is often saved with time and date stamps, as well as Global Positioning System coordinates. Police departments also use dashboard-mounted video cameras, or dash cams, to gather evidence during traffic stops and vehicle chases.

The use of body-worn cameras rose sharply after the 2014 police-involved shooting of Michael Brown in Ferguson, Missouri, when no video of that incident was available to corroborate or disprove Officer Darren Wilson's account. At the direction of President Obama, in 2015 the US Department of Justice launched a program that provided $75 million for police departments across the nation to purchase the devices. "Body-worn cameras hold tremendous promise for enhancing transparency, promoting accountability and advancing public safety for law enforcement officers and the communities they serve,"[27] the then attorney general Loretta Lynch said in 2015. Today surveys show that over 95 percent of American police departments use body cams.

There have been notable cases in which body-camera video evidence resulted in charges against a suspect being dropped or criminal charges being filed against a police officer for misconduct. In December 2017, for example, a Black man named Desmond Marrow was stopped by police in a suburb of Atlanta, Georgia, after a dispute with another driver. While arresting him, a White officer named David Rose placed his hands on Marrow's neck and choked him. After reviewing videos of the incident taken by the officer's dash cam and body cam, the Henry County Police Department fired Rose because he had violated department and county policies on the use of force.

> "Body-worn cameras hold tremendous promise for enhancing transparency, promoting accountability and advancing public safety for law enforcement officers and the communities they serve."[27]
>
> —Loretta Lynch, former US attorney general

Ferguson and the Emergence of Black Lives Matter

On August 9, 2014, police officer Darren Wilson shot eighteen-year-old Michael Brown during a struggle on the streets of Ferguson, Missouri. The incident sparked riots that lasted for weeks in Ferguson. Activists Alicia Garza, Patrisse Cullors, and Opal Tometi helped organize demonstrations and marches to protest Brown's death. They had previously used the social media hashtag #BlackLivesMatter in references to other cases, but the phrase gained national attention as the unrest in Ferguson lasted throughout August 2014.

Wilson was placed on leave while the incident was investigated by state and local authorities. However, in November 2014 a grand jury empaneled by the St. Louis County prosecutor's office, made up of six White and three Black residents, found that Wilson had acted in self-defense and declined to indict the officer. This touched off a new round of protests and riots in the city.

Over the next few years, Black Lives Matter grew into a national coalition with the goal of ending police violence toward racial minorities. The three founders worked to elect officials who believed in their cause. In 2018, with the support of Black Lives Matter, Wesley Bell became the first Black American elected as the St. Louis County prosecutor. He replaced longtime prosecutor Bob McCulloch, who had been criticized by Black Lives Matter for his handling of the Brown case. In early 2020 Bell reopened the case and spent five months reviewing the evidence to see whether Wilson should be charged with murder or manslaughter; however, in July Bell announced that no charges would be filed.

When Cameras Have Held Police Accountable

In another case, Officer Roy Oliver was convicted of murdering Jordan Edwards in Balch Springs, Texas. Edwards, a fifteen-year-old Black American, was one of five unarmed teens trying to drive away from a house party that police had raided. The police report of the incident initially said that the teens' vehicle drove "aggressively" toward Oliver's partner, Tyler Gross, forcing Oliver to fire five shots into the car. However, the police chief quickly withdrew the report and fired Oliver from the force when body-cam video showed the car moving away from the officers and not presenting any danger to either of them. After a jury convicted Oliver on murder charges in August 2018, the former officer was sentenced to fifteen years in prison.

These cases represent the results that advocates for Black and Hispanic communities expected from police body-cam programs. Many hoped that video evidence would make it easier to punish officers for using excessive force against people of color, but outcomes like Oliver's conviction are the exception, not the norm. "This is incredibly rare, it's really a historic moment," says veteran court reporter Jolie McCullough, who covered the Oliver case for the *Texas Tribune*. "Even in very high-profile shootings across the nation where there [has] been video . . . it's really hard to get a jury to decide to send a police officer—especially an on-duty police officer—to prison for something they were doing while they were on the job."[28]

In fact, an unforeseen consequence of body-cam programs is that the video is far more likely to be used by prosecutors as evidence in criminal trials, often against Black or Hispanic defendants, than it is to prosecute officers for police brutality. A recent study at George Mason University found that only about 8 percent of all cases in which body-worn camera video was introduced as evidence were prosecutions of police misconduct. More than 90 percent of body-cam videos were used to support criminal charges against civilians, a majority of whom were Black or Hispanic. Conse-quently, although public opinion polls show that Black Americans strongly support body-cam programs, many civil rights advocates have come to view the devices as tools for watching and control-ling communities of color, rather than as tools for preventing police brutality. "Body-worn cameras simply haven't served the interests of communities in most places, and primarily should be seen as a policing and surveillance tool,"[29] says Harlan Yu, executive director of the nonprofit civil rights organization Upturn.

> "Body-worn cameras simply haven't served the interests of communities in most places, and primarily should be seen as a policing and surveillance tool."[29]
>
> —Harlan Yu, executive director of Upturn

Cameras Are Only Part of a Solution

Even though dozens of civilian video recordings that show violent encounters between police and Black Americans are posted online every year, many Americans remain unwilling to believe that police act inappropriately when dealing with minorities. These people will search for ways to justify an officer's recorded actions, speculating that the victim might have been on drugs or had previously been involved in criminal activity. "You have people asking, 'well what happened before the camera started rolling? Did this person actually deserve their demise?'" notes Allissa V. Richardson, the author of *Bearing Witness While Black: African Americans, Smartphones and the New Protest #Journalism*. "African Americans in some ways are the only group that is asked to defend, or prove, or disprove, that they didn't hasten their own demise in some action that appeared off camera."[30]

Ahmaud Arbery's aunt listens as the family's attorney speaks with reporters after a hearing. The men who murdered Arbery might have gotten away with their crime if not for a cell phone video posted online.

Another concern, cautions Richardson, is that the large number of cell phone recordings released each year actually makes it easier for some people to dismiss allegations of police brutality any time they are *not* supported by video. In the absence of specific video evidence, many Americans tend to believe that police officers act responsibly and ethically all the time—despite the large volume of evidence to the contrary. Without a video, people are more likely to accept the official police report as factual, making it easier for authorities to cover up illegal activity.

The murder of Ahmaud Arbery, an unarmed Black man, provides a recent example of both how a cover-up can persist in the absence of video evidence and the power of video to achieve justice for victims of police brutality. On February 23, 2020, the twenty-five-year-old Arbery was jogging through a residential neighborhood in Glynn County, Georgia, when he was chased by three White men, shot, and killed. One of them was Gregory McMichael, a retired police officer and investigator for the county prosecutor's office. McMichael, his son Travis, and another man, William "Roddie" Bryan, were not arrested. Instead, the local prosecutor—who had worked with Gregory McMichael for many years—depicted Arbery as a potential burglar and said that McMichael and the others had been justified in shooting him. Despite public protests and national media attention, the case went nowhere for two and a half months. Then cell phone video taken by Bryan was posted online by local radio station WGIG. The video, which quickly went viral, showed Arbery being chased by the men in a white pickup truck, then being shot twice in the chest. The renewed public attention led state authorities to intervene in the case. Within two days, on May 7, 2020, the Georgia Bureau of Investigation had arrested the three White suspects, charging them with felony murder and aggravated assault. "This should have occurred the day it happened," Akeem Baker, one of Arbery's close friends, told the Associated Press after the arrests. "There's no way without the video this would have occurred. I'm just glad the light's shining very bright on this situation."[31]

CHAPTER 4

Holding Police Accountable

When police officers use excessive force against anyone, including minorities, they can be held criminally liable for their actions. In such cases, authorities have two options for criminal prosecution. Police officers can be tried for murder, manslaughter, or other serious charges in a state court. However, if authorities decline to bring charges, a state trial is dismissed, or the officers are exonerated at trial, then the US Department of Justice may investigate to determine whether the officer should be tried in federal court for a criminal violation of the victim's civil rights. State cases can usually be handled more quickly, so federal prosecutors often wait for the outcome of a state trial before initiating a federal civil rights case, which can take three years or more to resolve.

An example of how a lot of people expect the American criminal justice system to work occurred after the death of George Floyd in May 2020. The city of Minneapolis quickly fired the four officers involved in the incident. The Hennepin County district attorney filed criminal charges against Derek Chauvin, the officer who pressed his knee into Floyd's neck. After a week of community protests demanding stronger charges, the Minnesota attorney general took control of the case. In early June 2020 that office filed more serious charges of second-degree murder and manslaughter against Chauvin, as well as charging Alex Kueng, Thomas Lane, and Tou Thao with aiding and abetting Floyd's murder. The maximum penalty for those charges is a forty-year prison sentence. Federal prosecutors reported that they were also considering a criminal case against the four officers.

Few Officers Face Charges

Unfortunately, the Floyd case represents an exception, rather than the rule, when it comes to holding police criminally accountable. In most cases in which people are killed or injured by police officers using excessive force, prosecutors do not file criminal charges. There are several reasons for this. The "reasonableness" standard established in *Graham v. Connor* makes it harder for prosecutors to bring a case against police officers accused of using excessive force. In the nationally prominent police killings of Michael Brown, Eric Garner, and Tamir Rice, state and federal prosecutors ultimately said they did not have enough evidence to prosecute the officers. Criminal charges are even less likely in lower-profile cases, in which local prosecutors are often reluctant to charge police officers that they work with every day.

Philip Matthew Stinson, a professor at Bowling Green State University, has collected more than a decade's worth of data on excessive-force cases. In approximately ten thousand cases in which civilians were killed by police, Stinson found that only 153 officers (about 1.5 percent) faced criminal charges. Some of those officers pleaded guilty before going to trial. However, most officers whose cases went to trial ended up being acquitted. "It's rare that officers get prosecuted for on-duty deaths," Stinson told the *Washington Post*, "especially ones that are not shootings."[32]

> "It's rare that officers get prosecuted for on-duty deaths, especially ones that are not shootings."[32]
>
> —Philip Matthew Stinson, Bowling Green State University professor

In many other cases, when charges are filed against police officers, they are often for lesser crimes than manslaughter or second-degree murder. In the Breonna Taylor case, for example, Kentucky's attorney general filed criminal charges against only one of the seven officers who raided her apartment. Officer Brett Hankison was charged with wanton endangerment because several shots he fired went into a neighboring apartment where a White family lived—not because of Taylor's death.

"There's reluctance on the part of . . . prosecutors to hold police officers accountable because of the unique nature of the role they have," explains Michael Smith, a criminologist at the University of Texas at San Antonio. "There's a leeway that we typically want to give police, doing a difficult job under difficult circumstances. So there's a general reluctance for prosecutors to charge police for deaths in custody, and a reluctance for jurors to convict."[33]

An image on a protester's shirt shows former police officer Derek Chauvin kneeling on George Floyd's neck. Once these actions became known, Chauvin and the other officers involved in the incident were quickly fired.

I CAN'T BREATHE

Recourse in Civil Court

When authorities refuse to bring criminal charges, there is often just one other way for individuals or their families who believe police officers have violated their civil rights to receive justice. Title 42, Section 1983 of the US Code gives Americans the right to sue public officials who violate their rights and to collect monetary damages if their lawsuit is found to have merit. According to Section 1983, "Every person" who deprives another of the "rights, privileges, or immunities secured by the Constitution and laws, shall be liable to the party injured in an action at law, suit in equity, or other proper proceeding for redress."[34]

An important distinction between the civil and criminal court systems is that in the criminal system, the prosecutor brings the case on behalf of the state. The victim does little other than testify and receives no benefit other than the satisfaction of seeing the officer punished for inappropriate actions if convicted. Victims and their families have greater say in the process of a civil lawsuit. They can decide whether to accept a settlement or take the lawsuit to trial. The standard of evidence is also considerably lower for a civil trial; while criminal cases must be proved beyond a reasonable doubt, a defendant in a civil case will lose if the evidence indicates it is more likely than not that the defendant damaged the plaintiff (the person who filed the lawsuit) in some way.

Victims can seek both criminal and civil penalties simultaneously. In July 2020 George Floyd's family filed a civil lawsuit in federal court, seeking financial compensation from the four accused officers and the city government. "The city of Minneapolis has a history of policies, procedures and deliberate indifference that violates the rights of arrestees, particularly Black men, and highlights the need for officer training and discipline," commented civil rights attorney Benjamin Crump, who filed the suit on behalf of the Floyd family. Although the lawsuit did not specify the amount of damages, Crump said that the goal was to "make it financially prohibitive so police don't kill marginalized people and people of color."[35]

It is likely the Floyd family will receive some compensation, because communities have chosen to settle many other high-profile cases in which Black Americans died at the hands of police, rather than going through a civil trial. In 2015 New York City settled a lawsuit filed by the family of Eric Garner, paying $5.9 million, while Baltimore agreed to pay $6.4 million to the family of Freddie Gray. The next year, Cleveland paid $6 million to the family of Tamir Rice. In each of those settlements, the city did not admit any wrongdoing on the part of its police department. More recently, in September 2020 the city of Louisville announced that it had reached a settlement with the family of Breonna Taylor. In addition to paying $12 million, the city agreed to change procedures related to the use of search warrants and body cameras.

However, while large payouts like these make headlines, in many lower-profile cases the settlement amounts are much lower, sometimes amounting to as little as $7,500. And in almost all cases, it is the taxpayers who wind up footing the bill for police misconduct. Officers are typically covered under municipal insurance policies and rarely pay anything toward settlements. In addition, a controversial legal doctrine known as qualified immunity protects police officers and other government officials from being held liable for damages in civil lawsuits, unless their actions have specifically been found to be illegal in a very similar previous case.

In recent years Black leaders and civil rights advocates have called for the elimination of qualified immunity protections. Seeing officers who have killed or injured Blacks and Hispanics be permitted to resume work without consequence frustrates people of color, who consider this an example of a racist criminal justice system that allows police officers to get away with murder. "If officers know they

> "If officers know they have immunity, they act with impunity. If officers know they can unjustly take the life of a black person with no accountability, they will continue to do so."[36]
>
> —Benjamin Crump, civil rights attorney

After Louisville police killed Breonna Taylor, the city agreed to change its search warrant and body camera procedures. Taylor's family (her mother Tamika Palmer is pictured) also received $12 million.

have immunity, they act with impunity," Crump testified before the House Judiciary Committee in June 2020. "If officers know they can unjustly take the life of a black person with no accountability, they will continue to do so."[36]

The Origins of Qualified Immunity

In the 1961 case *Monroe v. Pape*, the Supreme Court established that civilians could sue police officers under Section 1983 of the US Code. Subsequently, during the 1960s the number of Section 1983 civil rights lawsuits exploded, rising more than 1,600 percent by the end of the decade. Concerned by this sharp increase, advocates for police contended that fear of being sued would cause police officers to second-guess themselves in dangerous situations. They also claimed that police departments would become bogged down in frivolous lawsuits and be unable to function properly. In response to these concerns, the Supreme Court introduced the doctrine of qualified immunity in the 1967 case

The Challenge of Firing Bad Police

Even in cases in which police officers do not receive qualified immunity, officers rarely face consequences for improper actions like using excessive force. In many municipalities, police unions have negotiated work rules that make it difficult to get rid of abusive officers. An investigation by the *Washington Post* found that nearly nineteen hundred officers were fired for misconduct from 2006 to 2017, but almost 25 percent of these officers ended up being reinstated after appeal. To improve accountability, the *Washington Post* claims all appeals must be more carefully reviewed.

Even when a department succeeds in getting rid of bad officers, their disciplinary records are often sealed, so they may be able to find another policing job. A 2020 study published in the *Yale Law Journal* focused on the phenomenon of "wandering officers," who are rehired as police after previously being fired for misconduct. The researchers found that each year, approximately 3 percent of all police officers in Florida fall into this category. Often, they wind up taking jobs with smaller police departments that are more likely to serve low-income communities with higher populations of color. The researchers found that these rehired officers tend to get into trouble at a higher rate than other officers. "When a wandering officer gets hired by a new agency, they tend to get fired about twice as often as other officers and are more likely to receive 'moral character violations,' both in general and for physical and sexual misconduct," comments study coauthor Ben Grunwald.

Quoted in Nikita Lalwani and Mitchell Johnston, "What Happens When a Police Officer Gets Fired? Very Often Another Agency Hires Them," *Washington Post*, June 16, 2020. www.washingtonpost.com.

Pierson v. Ray. The court ruled that government officials, including police officers, could not be sued if they were acting in "good faith."[37] This is the same legal standard that would protect officers from lawsuits if they had probable cause to detain or arrest someone and the person later turned out to be innocent.

The Supreme Court redefined the qualified immunity standard in the 1982 case *Harlow v. Fitzgerald*. Rather than relying on a good-faith defense, the court ruled in *Harlow* that police officers and other government officials are protected as long as their actions do not violate clearly established legal rights. To show that a right is clearly established, the plaintiff must identify a similar case that was previously decided either by the federal appellate court for that region or by the Supreme Court. If no such case can be identified, then the officer is immune from liability.

This has proved to be a challenging standard for plaintiffs to meet, and many Section 1983 lawsuits wind up being dismissed. The American Civil Liberties Union notes:

> "Under [the doctrine of qualified immunity] it is entirely possible—and quite common—for courts to hold that government agents *did* violate someone's rights, but that the illegality of their conduct wasn't well-established enough for them to be held liable."[38]
>
> —American Civil Liberties Union

Under this doctrine it is entirely possible—and quite common—for courts to hold that government agents *did* violate someone's rights, but that the illegality of their conduct wasn't well-established enough for them to be held liable. In practice, "clearly established law" is a very hard standard to meet. It generally requires civil rights plaintiffs to show not just a clear legal rule, but a prior case with very similar facts.[38]

Concerns About Qualified Immunity

There are legitimate reasons why public officials should be protected from the threat of frivolous lawsuits that could ruin them financially. In the majority opinion on *Harlow v. Fitzgerald*, Associate Justice Lewis F. Powell cited the "the expenses of litigation, the diversion of official energy from pressing public issues, and the deterrence of able citizens from acceptance of public office"[39] as reasons why society would benefit from providing this protection from liability to government officials.

However, civil rights advocates and police reformers point out that unlike most government officials, police officers carry

Associate Justice Sonia Sotomayor (pictured before she joined the US Supreme Court) has warned that the qualified immunity doctrine protects police officers at the expense of civil rights.

firearms and Tasers, have access to tear gas and military-grade weapons, and are authorized by the state to use force against civilians when necessary. With this power comes an obligation to discharge their duties responsibly and to be held accountable when they fail to do so. "It's one thing to say that public employees should generally be able to do their jobs without having to fear an onslaught of lawsuits," writes journalist Ian Millhiser, author of a book that discusses the impact of qualified immunity on communities of color. "It's another thing entirely to give sweeping legal immunity to people who are authorized by the state to inflict violence on citizens, and potentially even to take another person's life."[40]

Although the Supreme Court created the qualified immunity doctrine, in recent years justices have expressed reservations. Associate Justice Sonia Sotomayor has warned that the current doctrine protects police officers at the expense of civil rights. "We have not hesitated to summarily reverse courts for wrongly denying officers the protection of qualified immunity in cases involving the use of force," Sotomayor wrote in a 2017 opinion. "But we rarely intervene where courts wrongly afford officers the benefit of qualified immunity in these same cases."[41] In her dissent on the 2018 case *Kisela v. Hughes*, Sotomayor expanded on this idea:

A one-sided approach to qualified immunity transforms the doctrine into an absolute shield for law enforcement officers, gutting the deterrent effect of the Fourth Amendment. . . . It also sends an alarming signal to law enforcement officers and the public. It tells officers that they can shoot first and think later, and it tells the public that palpably unreasonable conduct will go unpunished.[42]

Suit and Countersuit in the Aftermath of Breonna Taylor's Death

In September 2020 Kenneth Walker, whose attempt to defend Breonna Taylor's apartment from intruders resulted in a deadly firefight with Louisville, Kentucky, police officers, filed a $10.5 million civil lawsuit against the city and its police department. Walker claimed in the suit that he had been falsely arrested and imprisoned the night of the police raid, that he had been assaulted and mistreated while in police custody, and that state charges filed against him for attempting to murder a police officer were meant to deflect attention from Taylor's death at the hands of police. (The state ended up dropping the charges in May.)

It seems likely that the individual police officers named in Walker's suit will receive qualified immunity, because the state attorney general's office has ruled their use of deadly force was justified. Taylor's family had previously sued the city, but Louisville agreed to pay a large settlement on behalf of all the public officials named in that lawsuit.

In October 2020 Sergeant Jonathan Mattingly filed a countersuit against Walker, seeking compensatory and punitive damages because, he alleged, Walker had shot him in the leg during the March 13 raid on Taylor's apartment. "Sgt. Mattingly [is] entitled to, and should, use the legal process to seek a remedy for the injury that Walker has caused him," his attorney, Kent Wicker, explained. Walker's attorney disagreed, calling Mattingly's lawsuit "the latest in a cycle of police aggression, deflection of responsibility, and obstruction of the facts in what is an obvious coverup."

Quoted in Elizabeth Joseph and Dakin Andone, "The Louisville, Kentucky, Police Officer Shot While Executing a Warrant at Breonna Taylor's Home Has Sued Her Boyfriend," CNN, October 30, 2020. www.cnn.com.

Despite such concerns, in recent years the Supreme Court has consistently refused to reconsider the doctrine of qualified immunity. Since 2015 the court has reversed more than a dozen appellate decisions and upheld officer requests for qualified immunity. And in June 2020 advocates were disappointed when the court decided not to hear nearly a dozen cases in which victims claimed that police had used excessive force.

Looking Ahead

With the Supreme Court unwilling to act, many observers believe it is up to Congress to resolve concerns about this doctrine with appropriate legislation. A provision in the George Floyd Justice in Policing Act, a bill introduced in Congress that contains many police reform measures, would make it more difficult for public officials to receive qualified immunity. That bill passed the House of Representatives in June 2020, but progress stalled in the Senate.

Several other bills have also focused on the issue. The Ending Qualified Immunity Act, introduced in the House of Representatives in June 2020, would require police officers involved in use-of-force incidents to cite a relevant law or court case to show how their action was in line with legal guidelines or past practices. Two similar pieces of legislation were introduced in the Senate during the summer of 2020.

"The principle at stake is simple: If citizens must obey the law, then government officials must obey the Constitution," points out Scott Bullock, president of the Institute for Justice. "The Constitution's promises of freedom and individual rights are important only to the extent that they are actually enforced."[43]

CHAPTER 5

Defunding the Police

In August 2020 the Minneapolis Charter Commission voted to take additional time reviewing a proposal by the city council to disband the police department. The proposal, passed unanimously by the council just weeks after the death of George Floyd, would have eliminated a provision in the city's charter that required it to operate and fund a police department. Council members proposed that police be replaced with a new Department of Community Safety and Violence Prevention, which would be responsible for "public safety services prioritizing a holistic, public health-oriented approach."[44] After the initial rush to make changes, however, the council has delayed amending the city's charter to acquire more input, especially from citizens. "It's appropriate to explore transformational changes in the department, but it needs to be done thoughtfully," says Commissioner Peter Ginder. "That hasn't been done here."[45]

But across the country, continuing protests by groups like Black Lives Matter have led many municipalities to reevaluate the ways that police departments operate and to consider reallocating police funding to other government agencies and programs. "A huge amount of public resources are put toward law enforcement agencies, at the expense of critical social services like education and health care," writes Black Lives Matter cofounder Patrisse Cullors. "This doesn't make us safer. . . . Investing in services like health care and education will reduce the role of police in society, protect Black lives, and shift the focus to helping people rather than harming them."[46]

Defunding the Police

The phrase "defunding the police" is controversial. Police supporters claim that the phrase implies eliminating police departments altogether, as Minneapolis's council has proposed. Conservative politicians raise fears that getting rid of police will result in anarchy. A Trump campaign advertisement that aired during the summer of 2020 draws on this fear, showing fires burning, people breaking windows and looting stores, and protesters holding signs reading "Defund the police." A recorded voice supposedly in response to a 911 emergency call passively states, "Due to defunding of the police department, no one is available to take your call."[47]

For many reformers, however, defunding does not necessarily mean eliminating police altogether. Instead, they believe that some police funding should be redirected from law enforcement activities to other local government agencies that provide community services like education, public health, drug rehabilitation, housing, job training, and youth programs. The idea, activists say, is that police are not properly trained for many nonviolent, noncriminal social issues that they are often asked to handle, such as dealing with the homeless or the mentally ill. Reallocating some police funding could allow government agencies to create teams of social workers, health care providers, and other specialists that could respond to these calls, freeing police officers to focus on criminal activities. Many of these commentators believe that spending on social services

"Investing in services like health care and education will reduce the role of police in society, protect Black lives, and shift the focus to helping people rather than harming them."[46]

—Patrisse Cullors, activist and Black Lives Matter cofounder

How Americans View Police Defunding and Other Reform Proposals

A July 2020 poll by the Gallup organization reveals that many Americans (58 percent) believe that major changes in policing are needed, but not all reforms have equal support. And support varies even more when the results are broken down by race and ethnicity. In all categories, abolishing police departments has the least support. However, about half of all Americans (and significantly more Black Americans) favor ending officer involvement in nonviolent crimes and shifting money from police departments to social programs.

Americans' Support for Policing Reform Options, by Race/Ethnicity

	All Americans	Black Americans	Asian Americans	Hispanic Americans	White Americans
Changing management practices so officers with multiple incidents of abuse of power are not allowed to serve	98%	99%	98%	99%	97%
Requiring officers to have good relations with the community	97%	97%	98%	96%	97%
Changing management practices so officer abuses are punished	96%	98%	99%	96%	95%
Promoting community-based alternatives such as violence intervention	82%	94%	91%	83%	80%
Ending stop and frisk	74%	93%	89%	76%	70%
Eliminating police unions	56%	61%	68%	56%	55%
Eliminating officer enforcement of nonviolent crimes	50%	72%	72%	55%	44%
Reducing the budgets of police departments and shifting the money to social programs	47%	70%	80%	49%	41%
Abolishing police departments	15%	22%	27%	20%	12%

Source: Steve Crabtree, "Most Americans Say Policing Needs 'Major Changes,'" Gallup, July 22, 2020.

and education would keep many individuals from ever engaging in potentially criminal behaviors that would require police intervention.

Rashawn Ray, a scholar with the Brookings Institution, writes:

One consistent finding in the social science literature is that if we really want to reduce crime, education equity and the establishment of a work infrastructure is the best approach. A study using 60 years of data found that an increase in funding for police did not significantly relate to a decrease in crime. Throwing more police on the street to solve a structural problem is one of the reasons why people are protesting in the streets. Defunding police . . . may be more beneficial for reducing crime and police violence.[48]

Reducing Inappropriate Responses

Police officers spend much of their shifts responding to nonemergency calls. In fact, some data suggests that up to 90 percent of all 911 calls do not involve violent situations, and a 2019 study found that police spend 21 percent of their time just answering calls involving people with mental health issues. Unfortunately, the way that police are trained tends to be counterproductive when it comes to dealing with the mentally ill. A recent *Washington Post* review of deadly force incidents found that one in four people killed by police officers suffered from a serious mental illness at the time of their death.

A recent example occurred in Rochester, New York, when a forty-one-year-old Black man named Daniel Prude was visiting his brother Joe's home in March 2020.

"Throwing more police on the street to solve a structural problem is one of the reasons why people are protesting in the streets. Defunding police . . . may be more beneficial for reducing crime and police violence."[48]

—Rashawn Ray, professor of sociology and fellow at the Brookings Institution

Black America's Attorney General

Benjamin Crump is widely recognized as the "go-to" lawyer for Black Americans who have been victimized by police brutality. At George Floyd's funeral, the Reverend Al Sharpton introduced Crump as "Black America's Attorney General."

Crump was born in Lumberton, North Carolina, in 1969, the oldest of nine children, and was raised by his mother and grandmother. As a child, he and other Black children were bused to an elementary school in a White neighborhood. He later said that the stark differences between the two communities motivated him to become a civil rights lawyer. Crump attended high school in Florida and earned a scholarship to Florida State University. He graduated with a law degree in 1995.

In 2012 Crump represented the family of Trayvon Martin, a Black teenager who was killed by a neighborhood watch member in Sanford, Florida. Crump skillfully used the media to draw national attention to the case and won a civil judgment against Martin's killer. Since then, he has been involved in many other high-profile cases involving police killings, representing the families of Michael Brown, Tamir Rice, Breonna Taylor, George Floyd, and Jacob Blake, among others. "I'm not stunned that this is happening in 2020," he told the *Washington Post*. "It takes extraordinary effort in America for black people to get simple justice. I feel like I'm running out of time."

Quoted in Karen Heller, "Ben Crump Has Become the Go-To Attorney for Racial Justice: 'I Feel like I'm Running Out of Time,'" *Washington Post*, June 19, 2020. www.washingtonpost.com.

Daniel had a history of mental illness; earlier in the day, the family had taken him to a hospital, fearing that he might hurt himself or commit suicide. Daniel was released from the hospital after a few hours and returned to his brother's home, where he continued acting erratically. Joe called 911, asking for help; he let the dispatcher know that Daniel was having a psychotic episode. When police arrived that snowy night, they found Daniel naked in the street despite the freezing temperatures, speaking incoherently.

Body-cam video of the encounter—which was not released by police until September 2020—shows that Daniel Prude lay down when ordered by police, was not armed, and did not resist when they handcuffed him. However, when he spit at officers, one of them placed a hood over his head, which caused the distraught man to panic. Officers then held Prude down for about three minutes. By the time an ambulance arrived, Prude had stopped breathing. Prude was revived, but he had suffered irreversible brain damage from lack of oxygen. He died in the hospital a week later.

"Everything that they did, they didn't have to do," an anguished Joe Prude later told National Public Radio. "That excessive force they used on him, the pushup stands on his neck, the knee on his back, holding his legs, that wasn't called for. . . . They treated my brother like he was an animal in the street. . . . I didn't call them to come help my brother die, I called them to come help me get my brother some help."[49]

Mental health professionals like Krystal Schulik, a counselor in Rochester, point out that the typical response by police is likely to make a situation worse when it involves someone who is mentally ill. Instead of handcuffs and hoods, she says, officers should speak calmly and reassuringly, reducing tension so that the person can be taken to a hospital for help without being hurt. "Change your tone of voice, your body language, you might have to get on the ground with him! Give him eye contact," Schulik says. "All of that is so important when deescalating such a scale of an event."[50]

How Defunding Might Work

Camden, New Jersey, offers some of the potential successes and pitfalls of a defunding model. Camden is a small city across the Delaware River from Philadelphia. More than 50 percent of Camden's eighty thousand residents are Hispanic, while 42 percent are Black. It has long been recognized as one of the poorest communities in the nation, with more than 40 percent of residents living below the poverty line.

A Virginia police dispatcher answers a 911 call. Many of the calls police respond to nationwide involve people with mental health issues rather than violent situations.

During the period from 2008 to 2012, Camden had the highest crime rate of any major US city. There were more than three thousand vacant homes and businesses, and drug dealers operated openly on street corners and empty lots. Camden also had serious financial problems. In 2010 a $14 million budget deficit forced the city to lay off half of its police force. The already high crime rate skyrocketed. Sixty-seven people were murdered in 2011, and burglaries increased by 65 percent.

The Camden police force's bad reputation compounded the problem. During 2010 and 2011, there were dozens of public complaints about excessive use of force by police. None were substantiated by police investigators, which the local American Civil Liberties Union affiliate and other watchdog groups claimed was evidence that chronic misbehavior was being covered up. Five Camden officers were convicted in 2010 of planting evidence and framing suspects in drug cases, but other corrupt officers were protected by a politically powerful police union.

Opinions on Defunding Police

A July 2020 poll by the Pew Research Center found that about 73 percent of Americans were opposed to defunding police in their local areas. Forty-two percent told Pew that they wanted to maintain local police spending at current levels, while 31 percent wanted spending to increase. Just 25 percent of respondents said that police spending should be reduced. Of that group, Black adults (42 percent) were twice as likely as White adults (21 percent) to favor cutting police budgets. Polls conducted by the *Washington Post*-ABC News and by the Gallup Organization found similar results. All three polls also indicated a wide generation gap on the issue. Regardless of race, adults under age forty were much more likely to support cutting police funding than were adults over forty.

Americans did agree almost universally on several proposals to reform police departments. For example, Pew found that 92 percent of Americans support requiring police to be trained in nonviolent alternatives to deadly force. Gallup found that 96 percent of Americans support changing practices and policies such as qualified immunity to ensure that police officer misconduct is punished, while 98 percent believe officers involved in such incidents should no longer be allowed to serve. And while defunding remains controversial, 82 percent of Americans support a greater role for community organizations in responding to some problems traditionally handled by police.

In 2012 New Jersey governor Chris Christie, key state legislators from both political parties, and local officials developed a plan to dissolve the city's police force and replace it with a new county police force. The plan was controversial, in part because the new county force would not be unionized. Former city officers could apply for jobs with the county police force, but most would earn less than they had under the city's union contract. Critics claimed that the plan was an effort to break the union; supporters pointed out that eliminating the union would allow the county to hire more officers. Some Camden residents even went to court to block the change. Despite their challenge, the city police force was disbanded in May 2013, and the new county police force was created.

For new police chief J. Scott Thomson, a lifelong city resident, the priority was to integrate officers into the community. Thomson changed the internal rating system for officers, who would no longer be rewarded based on the number of tickets written or arrests made. He implemented a system to investigate resident complaints and discipline officers who spoke disrespectfully or behaved inappropriately. Thomson later recalled telling Camden officers:

> I don't want you to write tickets, I don't want you to lock anybody up. I'm dropping you off on this corner that has [high] crime rates . . . and for the next 12 hours I don't want you to make an arrest unless it's for an extremely vile offense. Don't call us—we're not coming back to get you until the end of your shift, so if you got to go to the bathroom, you need to make a friend out here.[51]

Struggles and Successes

Despite Thomson's open approach, the county officers initially struggled to build trust with the community. During 2014 Camden led the state in the number of excessive force complaints, with sixty-five—more than the combined total of the two largest cities in New Jersey, Newark and Jersey City. Some Camden residents complained that the county police were writing many tickets for minor offenses.

"The significant increase in low-level arrests and summonses, combined with what appears to be the absence of adequate accountability for excessive force complaints, raise serious concerns," said Udi Ofer, American Civil Liberties Union of New Jersey executive director, in 2015. "The reality is that more people are being arrested for petty offenses, which is overwhelming the courts and has the potential to create a climate of fear, rather than respect, in the community."[52]

In response, Thomson made numerous adjustments. One change involved working with the Police Executive Research Forum, a respected policing organization in Washington, DC, that specializes in training police officers to end confrontations without resorting to deadly force.

The new training paid off quickly. In November 2015 police responded to reports of a man threatening customers with a knife at a fried chicken restaurant. When the man came outside, brandishing the knife, a dozen officers surrounded him in the street. The man ignored orders to drop his weapon and began walking down the street, slashing with the knife. But instead of drawing their own weapons, the officers maintained a cordon around the man until they had an opportunity to tackle him, then they took him into custody. The entire encounter—recorded on body cameras—took about ten minutes. "Similar scenarios have resulted in fatal shootings, often of unarmed people, but using time, distance and communication, the Camden Police Department de-escalated the potentially deadly situation,"[53] reports the *Washington Post*.

"If we approached that night with the old-guard mentality, we would have had an officer-involved fatal shooting," explains Thomson. He noted that the officers could legally have used deadly force to resolve the situation, but said that because of the new training "we would have walked with him for another mile. If there's something else [police] can do to avoid taking that person's life, there should be an obligation on us to exercise those options."[54]

In 2019 the Camden County Police Department implemented strict guidelines that clearly outline when deadly force can be used. The department's new policy was developed by New York

"If there's something else [police] can do to avoid taking [a] person's life, there should be an obligation on us to exercise those options."[54]

—J. Scott Thomson, former chief of the Camden County Police Department

Camden, New Jersey, police officers attend an award ceremony in 2019. The Camden police department implemented strict guidelines on when deadly force can be used.

University's Policing Project and approved by both the American Civil Liberties Union and the local police union. It even requires officers to intervene when they see another officer violating the policy. Since then, complaints of excessive use of force by the Camden police have dropped to fewer than five a year.

There Are No Easy Solutions

Since the new force was created, Camden has seen a 23 percent drop in violent crime and a 48 percent drop in nonviolent crime. However, observers close to the situation say that these statistics do not tell the whole story. The police force does not represent the racial diversity of the community, because most of the officers in Camden are White. Community activists drove the department to accept the new policy. And what worked in Camden will not necessarily translate to other communities.

Surely, no single reform or approach will eliminate the problem of police violence involving people of color. Still, opinion polls indicate a changing attitude about police and minorities and a greater willingness to address this challenging issue. In 2014, after the death of Michael Brown in Ferguson, Missouri, 43 percent of Americans said that the killing indicated a broad problem with policing, while 51 percent said it was just an isolated incident. In June 2020, 69 percent of Americans told a *Washington Post* poll that the killing of George Floyd indicated a broad problem, and 81 percent of Americans said police need to continue working to ensure fair treatment of Blacks. The mass protests that have been held across the country may produce enough public pressure for policy changes at the local, state, and federal levels. Hopefully, such changes will result in effective police departments that protect public safety while also respecting the rights of those they serve.

Introduction: Discriminatory Policing

1. Quoted in Associated Press, "George Floyd Transcript: Read It in Full Here," *Twin Cities* (St. Paul, MN), July 9, 2020. www.twincities.com.
2. Frank Edwards et al., "Risk of Being Killed by Police Use of Force in the United States by Age, Race-Ethnicity, and Sex," *Proceedings of the National Academy of Sciences*, August 2019. www.pnas.org.

Chapter 1: When Police Officers Use Force

3. Tennessee v. Garner, 471 U.S. 1 (1985).
4. Graham v. Connor, 490 U.S. 386 (1989).
5. Quoted in Rob Canning and Chad Lempe, "KY Police Officers Refer to 'Use-of-Force Continuum' When Subduing Subjects," WKMS, December 8, 2014. www.wkms.org.
6. Joseph Loughlin and Kate Flora, "Everything You Know About Police Shootings Is Wrong," *New York Post*, October 21, 2017. https://nypost.com.
7. Graham v. Connor.
8. Michael Ranalli, "Police Use of Force: The Need for the Objective Reasonableness Standard," Lexipol, March 24, 2017. www.lexipol.com.
9. Quoted in German Lopez, "Police Can Use Deadly Force If They Merely Perceive a Threat," Vox, November 14, 2018. www.vox.com.
10. Quoted in Lopez, "Police Can Use Deadly Force If They Merely Perceive a Threat."
11. Quoted in Ashley Fantz et al., "Tamir Rice Shooting: No Charges for Officers," CNN, December 28, 2015. www.cnn.com.

12. Quoted in Associated Press, "Tamir Rice: Family Releases Statement," *Jet*, December 28, 2015. www.jetmag.com.

Chapter 2: The Militarization of Police

13. Louisville Metro Police Department, "Criminal Interdiction Division." https://louisville-police.org/Directory.aspx?did=61.
14. Jonathan Blanks, "The War on Drugs Has Made Policing More Violent," *Democracy: A Journal of Ideas*, July 19, 2016. https://democracyjournal.org.
15. Michelle Alexander, *The New Jim Crow: Mass Incarceration in the Age of Colorblindness*. New York: New Press, 2012, p. 180.
16. Jonathan Mummolo, "Militarization Fails to Enhance Police Safety or Reduce Crime but May Harm Police Reputation," *Proceedings of the National Academy of Sciences*, August 20, 2018. www.pnas.org.
17. Quoted in "USA: Law Enforcement Violated Black Lives Matter Protesters' Human Rights, Documents Acts of Police Violence and Excessive Force," Amnesty International, August 4, 2020. www.amnesty.org.
18. Quoted in Katherine Hafner, "What Makes a Protest Turn Violent? Police in Riot Gear Can Be a Key Factor, Decades of Research Shows," *Virginian-Pilot* (Norfolk, VA), June 11, 2020. www.pilotonline.com.
19. Quoted in Hafner, "What Makes a Protest Turn Violent?"
20. Alex S. Vitale, "How to End Militarized Policing," *The Nation*, August 18, 2014. www.thenation.com.
21. Quoted in Alice Speri et al., "The George Floyd Killing in Minneapolis Exposes the Failures of Police Reform," The Intercept, May 29, 2020. https://theintercept.com.

Chapter 3: Filming the Police

22. Quoted in Nicole Chavez, "What We Know So Far About Jacob Blake's Shooting," CNN, August 27, 2020. www.cnn.com.
23. Eugene Robinson, "We Need Black Lives Matter. The Police Who Shot Jacob Blake Prove It," *Washington Post*, August 24, 2020. www.washingtonpost.com.

24. American Civil Liberties Union of Illinois v. Anita Alvarez, No. 11-1286 (7th Cir. 2012).
25. Palika Makam, "How to Safely and Ethically Film Police Misconduct," *Teen Vogue*, June 12, 2020. www.teenvogue.com.
26. Makam, "How to Safely and Ethically Film Police Misconduct."
27. Quoted in David Jackson, "Obama Team Will Fund Police Body Camera Project," *USA Today*, May 1, 2015. www.usatoday.com.
28. Quoted in Rhonda Fanning, "Body Camera Footage Led to Rare Murder Conviction for a Balch Springs Police Officer," Texas Standard, August 29, 2018. www.texasstandard.org.
29. Quoted in Louise Matsakis, "Body Cameras Haven't Stopped Police Brutality. Here's Why," *Wired*, June 17, 2020. www.wired.com.
30. Quoted in Tonya Mosley, "How Technology Plays a Role in Advancing Civil Rights for Black Americans," *Here & Now*, WBUR, June 8, 2020. www.wbur.org.
31. Quoted in Russ Bynum and Ben Nadler, "Father, Son Charged with Killing Black Man Ahmaud Arbery," Associated Press, May 8, 2020. https://apnews.com.

Chapter 4: Holding Police Accountable

32. Quoted in Tom Jackman and Devlin Barrett, "Charging Officers with Crimes Is Still Difficult for Prosecutors," *Washington Post*, May 29, 2020. www.washingtonpost.com.
33. Quoted in Jackman and Barrett, "Charging Officers with Crimes Is Still Difficult for Prosecutors."
34. 42 U.S. Code § 1983.
35. Quoted in KARE-11 News, "Floyd Family Sues City of Minneapolis, Officers Charged in His Death," July 14, 2020. https://www.kare11.com.
36. Quoted in Benjamin Siegel and Libby Cathey, "'Stop the Pain': George Floyd's Brother Testifies on Policing Reform," ABC News, June 10, 2020. https://abcnews.go.com.
37. Pierson v. Ray, 386 U.S. 547 (1967).
38. American Civil Liberties Union, "Baxter v. Bracey," July 2, 2020. www.aclu.org.

39. Harlow v. Fitzgerald, 457 U.S. 800 (1982).
40. Ian Millhiser, "Why Police Can Violate Your Constitutional Rights and Suffer No Consequences in Court," *Vox*, June 3, 2020. www.vox.com.
41. Quoted in Marcia Coyle, "At Supreme Court, Sotomayor Is Leading Voice Against Alleged Police Abuses," *National Law Journal*, June 3, 2020. www.law.com.
42. Kisela v. Hughes, 584 U.S. 17-467 (2018).
43. Quoted in Nick Sibilla, "End Qualified Immunity," Institute for Justice, June 25, 2020. https://ij.org.

Chapter 5: Defunding the Police

44. Quoted in Vanessa Romo, "Minneapolis Council Moves to Defund Police, Establish 'Holistic' Public Safety Force," National Public Radio, June 26, 2020. www.npr.org.
45. Quoted in *New York Post*, "Proposal to Disband Minneapolis Police Blocked from Ballot," August 5, 2020. https://nypost.com.
46. Patrisse Cullors, "'Black Lives Matter' Is About More than the Police," American Civil Liberties Union, June 23, 2020. www.aclu.org.
47. Quoted in *Cedar Rapids (IA) Gazette*, "Fact Checker: Trump's '911 Call' Ad Is Powerful, but Is It True?," August 17, 2020. www.thegazette.com.
48. Rashawn Ray, "What Does 'Defund the Police' Mean and Does It Have Merit?," *FixGov* (blog), Brookings Institution, June 19, 2020. www.brookings.edu.
49. Quoted in Christianna Silva, "Joe Prude Remembers His Brother Daniel Following His Death in Police Custody," *Morning Edition*, National Public Radio, September 4, 2020. www.npr.org.
50. Quoted in Eric Westervelt, "Mental Health and Police Violence: How Crisis Intervention Teams Are Failing," *All Things Considered*, National Public Radio, September 18, 2020. www.npr.org.
51. Quoted in Katherine Landergan, "The City That Really Did Abolish the Police," *Politico*, June 12, 2020. www.politico.com.

52. American Civil Liberties Union, "Policing in Camden Has Improved, but Concerns Remain," May 18, 2015. www.aclu.org.

53. Deanna Paul, "Police Must First Do No Harm: How One of the Nation's Roughest Cities Is Reshaping Use-of-Force Tactics," *Washington Post*, August 21, 2019. www.washingtonpost.com.

54. Quoted in Paul, "Police Must First Do No Harm."

ORGANIZATIONS AND WEBSITES

American Civil Liberties Union (ACLU)

www.aclu.org

Founded in 1920, the ACLU focuses on pursuing legal actions on civil rights issues and most recently has been campaigning for police reform. By accessing the link for Racial Justice on the organization's website, visitors can learn about court cases the ACLU has filed against city police departments seeking justice for victims of police misconduct.

Communities United for Police Reform

www.changethenypd.org

Communities United for Police Reform is an organization of residents and activists from the five boroughs of New York City dedicated to ending discriminatory policing practices. The site includes links to news articles as well as resources to help people understand their rights when observing police misconduct.

Fraternal Order of Police

www.fop.net

The Fraternal Order of Police is the world's largest organization of sworn law enforcement officers, with more than 355,000 members. The organization is committed to improving the working conditions for law enforcement officers and the safety of those they serve. The website includes information on FOP programs and training.

The Movement for Black Lives

https://m4bl.org

The Movement for Black Lives is a diverse coalition of more than fifty organizations that represent the interests of Black communities throughout the United States. A guide to legal resources, along with information about upcoming events and informative articles about how to support the movement, can be found on the official site.

National Police Accountability Project (NPAP)

www.nlg-npap.org

The NPAP is a nonprofit organization created by the National Lawyers Guild to promote the accountability of law enforcement officers and police departments that violate the Constitution and laws of the United States. The site provides background on the NPAP's legislative effort to eliminate qualified immunity for police officers, as well as other useful information.

Office of Community Oriented Policing Services (COPS Office)

https://cops.usdoj.gov

COPS Office is a branch of the US Department of Justice that dispenses information to the public and police to address crime. The Collaborative Reform Inititative link in the center of the web page provides information about federal grants to improve the practices of state, local, and tribal law enforcement agencies.

FOR FURTHER RESEARCH

Books

Thomas Abt, *Bleeding Out: The Devastating Consequences of Urban Violence and a Bold New Plan for Peace in the Streets*. New York: Basic Books, 2019.

Radley Balko, *Rise of the Warrior Cop: The Militarization of America's Police Forces*. New York: Perseus, 2013.

Paul Butler, *Chokehold: Policing Black Men*. New York: New Press, 2018.

Christopher J. Lebron, *The Making of Black Lives Matter: A Brief History of an Idea*. New York: Oxford University Press, 2017.

Joseph Loughlin and Kate Flora, *Shots Fired: The Misunderstandings, Misconceptions, and Myths About Police Shootings*. New York: Skyhorse, 2017.

Khalil Gibran Muhammad, *The Condemnation of Blackness: Race, Crime, and the Making of Modern Urban America*. Cambridge, MA: Harvard University Press, 2019.

Barbara Ransby, *Making All Black Lives Matter: Reimagining Freedom in the Twenty-First Century*. Oakland: University of California Press, 2018.

Internet Sources

Jonathan Blanks, "The War on Drugs Has Made Policing More Violent," *Democracy: A Journal of Ideas*, July 19, 2016. https://democracyjournal.org.

Patrisse Cullors, "'Black Lives Matter' Is About More than the Police," American Civil Liberties Union, June 23, 2020. www.aclu.org.

Scott DuFour, "Us Versus Them in Policing: What Causes Warrior Cops?," In Public Safety, May 15, 2019. https://inpublicsafety.com.

Kimberly Kindy, "Creating Guardians, Calming Warriors: A New Style of Training for Police Recruits Emphasizes Techniques to Better De-Escalate Conflict Situations," *Washington Post*, December 10, 2015. www.washingtonpost.com.

Robert Muggah and Thomas Abt, "Calls for Police Reform Are Getting Louder—Here Is How to Do It," *Foreign Policy*, June 22, 2020. https://foreignpolicy.com.

Lynne Peeples, "What the Data Say About Police Brutality and Racial Bias—and Which Reforms Might Work," *Nature*, June 19, 2020. www.nature.com.

INDEX

PICTURE CREDITS

ABOUT THE AUTHOR

Jim Gallagher is the author of more than twenty books for young adults. The titles, written for various publishers, include *The Johnstown Flood*, *Causes of the Iraq War*, *Illegal Immigration*, and *Refugees and Asylum*. He lives in central New Jersey with his wife, LaNelle, and their three children.